THIS BOOK BELONGS TO

Made in the USA
Monee, IL
20 February 2022

91524575R00057